# COLD
## TO THE BONE

To Holly,

Enjoy!

*[signature: John B...]*

**POEMS BY JOHN BATES**

## Other Books by John Bates

*Trailside Botany* ©*1995*

*Seasonal Guide to the Natural Year: Minnesota, Michigan, and Wisconsin* ©*1997*

*A Northwoods Companion: Spring and Summer* ©*1997*

*A Northwoods Companion: Fall and Winter* ©*1997*

*A River Life: The Natural and Cultural History of a Northern River* ©*2001*

*Graced by the Seasons: Spring and Summer in the Northwoods* ©*2006*

*Graced by the Seasons: Fall and Winter in the Northwoods* ©*2008*

## Contributing Author

*Harvest Moon* ©*1993*

*A Place to Which We Belong: Wisconsin Writers on Wisconsin Landscapes* ©*1999*

*Seasons of the North* ©*2003*

*White Deer* ©*2007*

*Stories from the Shore* ©*2007*

*Pure Superior* ©*2009*

*Wildbranch: An Anthology of Nature, Environmental, and Place-based Writing* ©*2010*

# COLD
## TO THE BONE

JOHN BATES

Manitowish River Press

**Cold to the Bone**

© 2017 by John Bates. All rights reserved.

Book and cover design: Carole Sauers/Penny Lane Studio

Cover photo: Jacquard weavings by Mary Burns

Bates, John, 1951-

*Cold to the Bone* written by John Bates;
Jacquard weavings by Mary Burns

ISBN  978-0-9656763-7-3 (softcover)

Library of Congress Control Number: 2017934290

Manitowish River Press
4245N State Highway 47
Mercer, WI 54547
*www.manitowish.com*

Printed in the United States of America

10 9 8 7 6 5 4 3 2 1

# TABLE OF CONTENTS

## WATER

# WOODS

# HOME

*To my best friend,
my partner in botany and birding
and paddling and exploring the world,
in all things creative and meaningful,
my wife, Mary.*

WATER

# PANDEMONIUM

The frogs are chorusing tonight.
The peepers chime like ten thousand sleigh bells
rung by ecstatic Salvation Army volunteers.
Meanwhile, the toads trill at diverging pitches,
harmonizing in drones like a hall of chanting Buddhists.

All night they sing.
Whenever I wake up, they're still there
in the dark and the damp
under the moon and stars
stagelighting their Dionysian debauch.

I have tried to sneak up on them
to witness the passion that has brought them,
and their thousands of generations before,
to these ephemeral ponds.

But even in their single mindedness,
they always hear me
and go stone quiet.

If I wait long enough,
one will give in to his need for a mate
and begin singing again.
Then the choral dam breaks,
and the din commences
because it must.

It's a game of Russian roulette,
this fertilizing of eggs.
The bet is that the pools won't dry up
before the great metamorphosis,
from fins to legs
from gills to lungs
from water to forest.

All this.
Then, without apparent discussion,
they agree to gather here again,
next spring,
when a south wind will warm air and water
triggering their tumultuous voices
like a thousand drunken guests at a lavish wedding party
breathing rapture in the dark spring night.

# IF YOU LISTEN

If you listen –
you may be amazed.

It depends on what you brought to the shore.

It changes for me every time.
The other day I brought the memory of a neighbor
who said something I didn't like
and now I've made it a hit song,
number one on my playlist.
And so I couldn't see the lake that day,
even though it was right there.

But the next day, the wind was picking up the lily leaves
and waving them,
along with the bulrushes which were bowing again and again
by the thousands, I swear!
in a great surging buoyancy
and I felt
like they were carrying me to the shore,

where, if I wanted,
I could jump on the backs of the tall grasses
with a smile as broad as the rippling prairie,
the prairie which races in undulations,
undulations that if they were chords of music
would carry me away singing to the Pacific,

where,
I remember now,
I visited in my boyhood.
The ocean was full of diving terns, circling pelicans, whales spouting
all the world coming and going
and all I had to do,
just like here,
where ospreys dive, cranes sail, sturgeons jump,
was watch,
was listen.

# BOG WALKING

Stepping barefoot onto the bog mat,
the ground is now a joyful unfamiliarity,
undulating in response to my movement
like a dance partner
like a stone dropped in the water.

The water oozes ice cold around my ankles,
the moss cushioning my steps
compressing-expanding,
exhaling-inhaling
like a colossal sponge
like an echo.

It's quiet out here.
I'm looking for rose pogonias
with their fringed tongues.

But what I really want to find
are dragon's mouth orchids.

The name alone entices me –
a dragon hiding in all this cold and wet and acid.
Imagine a dragon's mouth . . . red fire, black tongue.

This is why I like botanists,
they with their Latin names and terminology,
but their imaginations still as playful
as the bog mat itself,
still as colorful as the many shades
of red and yellow and green
that the sphagnum has imagined into life,
still as open to strange possibility
as the dark water
in the center of the bog
where a blue-winged teal rests,
the luminous crescent moon
reflected
in front of its eyes.

# LOOKING

Mist rises in the early evening
over the river
under the full moon.

Spring peepers crescendo in the reeds,
great horned owls baritone from the wood edge,
woodcocks skydance for a mate.

I stand on the old bridge.

A muskrat vees upstream.

A mallard pair muddle in the slough.

Two eagles fly low
surprisingly softly
back to their nest.

The night sifts in,
stars emerge,
tremble,
the Milky Way opens.

The white pines grow larger.

Sight dissolves within sounds and smells,
and soon a cold dampness seeps through.

I am content just here,
my wandering spirit
temporarily stilled,
here
where the mist over the river
holds universe enough.

# COUNTING FROGS

In April, then May, then June
we count frogs.
The scientists have a protocol –
ten stops, five minutes at each place to listen,
rank them by overlapping calls, move on.

If there's been a drought, only a minute is needed.
But sometimes,
the best times,
we linger for a while,
not for the frogs who we count quickly,
but for the whip-poor-will who knows one thing,
and desires all others to know it, and only it.
For the snipe and the nighthawk
who contort the air into something unearthly
by knowing the physics of wind shear on feathers.
For the woodcock, stubby little strutter,
whose song on the ground is more insect than bird,
but who leaps into the air and flutters to a height
where he utters a twittering syncopation
that speaks of all awakenings.
For the beaver as it cruises by hidden in the dark water
and WHACKS its tail,
startling the bejeesus out of us.
For the loon far out on the lake
first tremeloing,
then yodeling, again and again,
until silence tells us the trouble is over
but not who won or who even survived.
For the barred owls who converse over the marsh
ending each thought with a wild drawl.
For the hermit thrush who speaks of heaven one last time
before the dark swallows his prayer.

For the occasional coyotes who suddenly yip
crazying the world.
For the simple plinks and plunks and plops of fish and ducks and turtles.
For the wind that rises in the pines and shivers the needles.
For all the stars that blink in as the dark deepens.
For the wavewash on the sand
For the moon on the water which stagelights it all.

. . .

...

These mysteries all send us into whispering amazement,
into standing closer to one another,
into bewildered small smiles
head shakes and shrugs
of what do you suppose that was?

Meanwhile, the frogs
may still be peeping or droning or gurgling or twanging,
each a foreign language among so many others,
all full of intention.

Back home, we dutifully fill out forms,
but the numbers say only a little about
what we really heard
or what finally matters.

# ANCIENT WATER

At dawn, the soft fog
laying on the water,
I swear I hear ancient voices
where the pale sun
burns the fog away.

Such an odd expression - "burning fog."

Where the river becomes Spider Lake
archeologists have found layers of lives
stacked on top of one another
like tree rings.

Here broken tools
date who they might have been
and why they might have lived here.

Right here in this place
and not somewhere else
in this plentiful world.

In the fog are other exhalations;
8,000 years of people,
yes,
but also otters, sandpipers,
pickerelweed, mussels,
all the lived life
on this ancient water.

A flock of geese suddenly emerge overhead,
their voices sewing continuity,
as do the voices of cranes
and spring peepers.
And then the blue heron appears,
fishing the meander
I've just come around,
a vein of river
which has wandered tirelessly,
but has ended up here
now
with this heron on its banks
with me in this canoe
in the burning fog.

# DINOSAURIAN
# GUMBALL MACHINES

(a phrase from Chet Raymo in *Natural Prayers*)

She lumbers into our driveway
having divined there is sand,
and begins digging.
Others of her kind emerge from creeks, marshes, lakes,
and crawl upslope to find other sand
along abandoned train tracks, on dikes, in logging roads.
Anywhere is good where sun and sand can brood
a nest of eggs for three months
like a pregnant mother might
were she able to birth 20 children at a time.
I wonder, is there a shared one-mindedness
among the shelled siblings?
a turtle telepathy
that lifts them from their wild solitude
into community?

They'll jailbreak in September
knowing somehow what direction is up
emerging and scrambling
in a beeline for the nearest water
like little half dollars with green legs and a GPS.

If the summer has been too wet and cool,
they will hatch later,
then discuss their options,
perhaps vote to stay in the nest until spring.

A slight problem will arise –
they will freeze nearly solid into turtlecubes,
turtlesickles if you prefer.
No breath, no heartbeat, no brain activity.
We call this D-E-A-D.

. . .

...

They call it something else,
because on a foggy evening in April
when the frost is out of the ground,
about the time the spring peepers begin their pandemonium,
the hatchlings, now 8 months old,
wake and dig,
not having eaten or grown even a millimeter,
not having lived really.
Instead, they experienced death after birth,
so they are ancestors of a sort
to themselves,
an oddity perhaps even to the turtle brain.

I doubt they are greeted at the shoreline as long lost relatives
who were left behind to emigrate home.

They just walk into the water,
each alone,
and begin swimming.

# COMING AWAKE

*How you stand here is important.*
*How you listen for the next thing to happen.*
*How you breathe.*
– William Stafford

You can't think of everything in one moment.
That's why you come back to places,
to open your heart,
to see what happens
this time.

When you come back,
you hope you left behind all the other things –
the anger,
the bitterness,
the judgment,
and brought the memories that matter –
the kindnesses.

Everyone sees something different here.
I have seen luminous things –
the stars glistening in the damp crescent-moon-air,
the bark canoes edging through the dawn fog,
the people happy in the rice beds.

And I've seen nothing.

This is a good place to fall asleep
in the warm bay,
the waves softly slapping the sand,

and then

to come awake.

# DISTRACTION DISPLAY

This morning a hen merganser
rushed across the water in front of our canoe
flailing wildly
as she feigned an injured wing.

This thespian performance
was given in honor of her chicks
who were huddled
in the long-stemmed bulrushes.

Her display was perfected long ago
to draw danger upon herself
in a trade for peace
upon her offspring,
and the continuity of her species.

And if she dies in the drama?
She will have paid the price expected.

I wonder if she understands the meaning of her sacrifice,
understands how perfectly it renders love
into a purity of action,
understands how inspirational such a simple act
can be upon an open heart.

# *ICE*

I went through the ice today
only up to my knee
and just one leg.
But my snowshoe was pinned under something in the muck
and I couldn't get out.
I pulled and pulled until my heart raced
like a snowshoe hare with a coyote on its tail.

And then I just stopped.

I looked around.
It was perfectly quiet in the alders.
The marsh water was black around my leg.
My dog sat close by, watching me, patient.

I wondered if in her DNA she knew who Lassie was.

I was close to home
but not so close that my shouts could be heard.
One option was to reach down in the icy muck
and try to unstrap my snowshoe.
But I didn't want it to become part of the archaeological record.
And I was afraid my fingers would freeze trying to undo the buckle.
So, rather than fighting to lift my leg,
I worked the long shoe back and forth, back and forth,
trying to carve away at the suction
and the branches that ensnared me.

I remembered then the conversation I had with my trapper friend
when he told me how he was trapping coyotes
and by mistake snared a male wolf in one of his traps.
He was proud that the trap had not injured the wolf's leg.
He called a wildlife manager who radio-collared the wolf,
and then they followed the wolf's signal every day for a week
until the signal went flat
and they found the wolf curled up,
shot to death.

. . .

...

I thought how if I was a coyote or wolf in a trap,
I would now lay down in the snow and wait
until someone approached and shot me.

Meanwhile, I was still working my shoe back and forth,
and slowly it came free
encased in black slush.
And I realized then that I was gulping breath
though I thought I was calm.
Just a little mishap in the ice.

And then I thought this:
that one is finally alone
and that the natural world is utterly indifferent

even though we love one another.

# MORNING ON THE RIVER

As dawn rinses the black heavens away,
and satin pink unfolds,
an eagle perches in the old flagged pine
beside the river.

Below the eagle,
the marsh resonates with primal calls
and slowly goldens,
shaking out the reflected stars
from its black water.

A blue luster creeps between the cattails,
tapping shoulders with the gold.

Songs rise on the morning curtain,
each in its appointed thrush time
according to sparrow light,
warbler heat,
all carrying on the wind and flow.

Then the sun backlights an eagle
as its silhouette falls
from a naked limb,
gliding on the uplifting hands
of rising heat.

Instantly all songs cease.
The shadow plunges,
raking the river's surface
yellow talons emerging . . .

empty.

Reluctant to give of itself this time,
the river pushes on,
no gain,
no loss,
just blue with sky,
white with clouds.

# IN THE BLACK MUCK

In the black muck
the rice has risen,
arched high like prairie grass on Kansas loam.

Not long ago on this shore
Ojibwa danced the rice,
their singing carrying over to the nearby lakes,
meeting other ricing songs
also on the wind.

They roasted the rice over fires
of maple, oak, birch.
Then they tossed little clouds of rice up into the wind,
the rice rising and falling from the baskets,
the puffs of chaff disappearing
within the trails of the smoking fires.

All of this happened
amidst the constant chattering of blackbirds,
which arrived today in clouds,
as they surely have for thousands of years,
all cousins and aunts and uncles,
all coming to gluttonize the rice.

Friends will collect 100 pounds of rice today,
their single mindedness necessary
to cook wild rice stews in January.

We, on the other hand,
will gather some
that we won't bother to weigh
and which we won't eat.
Later, we'll toss the seeds into another riverbed
and hope for the rice to rise from the muck
next spring.

After all, we're in a heaven of distractions.
The wind, the songs,
the clouds, the dreams,
weigh nothing.

# MUSKRATS

Venus glows above the landing.
We slide our canoe into the black water,
the aluminum grating on the pebble shore.

We paddle upstream through the cape of darkness
that melds river and bank.
The slough ice suddenly shatters,
and the stars glimmer on the shards.

In the silence and cold of late October
life is expressed in the quiet
splashes and the widening circles
of the wakes of animals headed home.

Even our softened voices are thunderstrikes.

We pull for the muskrat houses where the traps
vise the young and the old
who were wary of mink,
but not of metal jaws hidden
in their runways.

The East colors gradually in waves.
The muskrat houses emerge out of the dark waters
in gray to brown to salmon
to the tan of cattail and bulrush,
the interior of the hummocks constructed
into a room for eight
to wait out the months of ice.

We carefully count as we pull the traps –
33 houses, 67 traps, 24 dead muskrats,
four alive with broken legs,
each dispatched with a paddle blow
to a thin skull.
Two eaten by mink or owl
surely pleased by a prey
tethered to its home.

. . .

...

For tomorrow's catch, we tear
the walls of the houses,
the plungehole exits,
the feeding platforms,
and place our traps.
The muskrats will try to repair the tears,
but drowning awaits.

Three bald eagles observe from high pines.

As the morning grows, the wind comes up,
sweeping the wet lands of their darkness.
The marsh awakes with a rush of air
where sound had earlier ridden
freely on the dark balm.

We become efficient.
Each man performs his task in context,
the script executed.

Later, the trapper demonstrates
how to skin a muskrat in less than a minute,
the fur lifting with ease
as if it had been a coat all along.
A snip and cut from the back ankles to the anus,
and the pelt pulls over the head.
Then a snip at the front feet and jaws,
and the skin peels away.
It is as easy as taking off a sweater,
as easy as opening the housing of his outboard,
only now he exposes
the red machinery of the marsh.

# LATE APRIL

Late April when the sun's rays suddenly warm,
the snowmelt comes fast
and then we're awash in water,
the little streams gorged,
spilling over banks,
into the woods,
the wetlands,
a spring tsunami of water
pulsing everywhere.

The air saturates,
and fog drips,
so damp it's like wearing a wet rag.
Then the frost goes out of the ground
and it's mud season
when everything slurries.

Now little rivulets cascade through the hills
rushing on to Lake Superior,
water spilling everywhere,
everything running down,
down,
all different sounds
as the water rumbles over rocks
and is a softness through the leaves.

Forest, lake, river all meet,
mingling the mud and leaves and branches and stones,
all in one pulse
that will last into mid-May
when
the warblers and the wildflowers
will announce a halt
to the trains of water.
Everything will then settle in its new place
ready for the green-up,
the transformation
of sun, soil, water
into spring.

# COLD TO THE BONE

Through the mist and buffeting wind
the long-billed curlews beat their way
up and down the meanders,
at times hard against the wind's pulse,
at times careening with it,
either way fighting for control

then landing with a grace
that says
while there is always struggle,
we were made in the same house as the wind.

The grebe diving midstream,
the mallards sheltering in the shoreline sedges,
the rail pacing the thatched bank,
the sandpipers probing the muck,
each finds its way through this day,
each just as likely to be resting
with its bill tucked into its feathers
as to be a meal for a peregrine
which flashes by us in a laser-line,
streaming into the swallowing gray.

Slow of foot,
mist in our eyes,
cold to the bone,
we delight in every moment among them,
as we also delight to depart
back to roofs, windows, heat,
and a box lunch with food from other soils and waters and winds
that once too provided a home
to wildness
but were traded at a cost.

What other trade could we have done?
What else can we do?
Slow-footed,
mist in our eyes,
cold to the bone.

# MEANDERS

Mid-April dawn, spring snow falling,
wind fast-dancing the trees.
and we're paddling the river.
At first we surprise ducks who leap from the water,
and then the winter wren sings
in a wild jumbling grace that makes us both laugh,
so that when he stops,
we hear the silence for the first time.

It's 28 degrees.
We're crazy cold.
Our gloved hands clumsily lift our binoculars
as we round every bend
noticing newly formed back bays
where the river flooded,
where the trumpeter swans seem happy
in the opulence.

In the current's hand,
we're supposed to be counting cranes,
but the science gets lost
in the subtleties discovered
as the light sharpens.

We breathe deeper.
We hear distant bird songs
riding the edges of the wind,
hear the wild thrum
streaming from each swan's wingbeat
as three fly just overhead,
hear the raven's
bantering crazy oratory.

The swirling floodwaters first rinse the soils,
then sink in,
so the summer droughts can be scorned.

At the landing,
we pull out our data sheet,
now an afterthought,
and remember to add
two cranes.

# OVER THE BANK

As soon as the ice goes off in April,
we paddle the little river
now grown into full flood.
The lush wetlands of summer,
once all tall sedges and grasses,
are now a glimmering sheet,
a momentary lake,
the river lost in a blue abundance.

The ducks are happy.
They just arrived from their southern anywheres
where open water and peace prevailed.

In a few weeks, the water will recede,
revealing an immigrant personality,
the river now cutting new meanders,
perhaps cleaving an oxbow lake
or widening a loop
like a seamstress
pulling out her thread to try a new stitch.

The swimming hole on a deep corner of the river
where Mary's mother swam as a girl
is long gone,
consumed by a spring flood,
the river choosing another story line,
a novel flourish.

Does the river write joyfully, playfully, sadly?
It's hard to know what a little river in annual flood feels.
This isn't a powerful, hungry, raging flood.
Just a rising,
and then a settling.
A calm reordering.
A spilling over
and then a discovery
of what no one could have foreseen.

# IMMIGRATIONS

At the airport, people were deplaning from all parts of this world,
brilliant wardrobes flowing,
when over the multi-hued planes
a great blue heron
winged its slow way into the red setting sun.

And I wondered,
is there an Ellis Island for migrating birds?
a Statue of Liberty?
maybe a pretty chamber of commerce brochure
full of half-truths and glory
that birds dream of just before
they lift off into the half-light?

Next week back home,
birds streamed along Lake Superior's shoreline,
wary of the crossing,
but needing to find a way.
For them, shores are frontiers,
barriers,
launch pads.
Here the birds enter a world
where magnetism, sun, moon, stars, landscape,
transform from abstractions
into one map lit bright.

Do the birds find some transcendence
where mind body wind unite?
where they do an abracadabra act
– a swirl of wand, a little smoke –
and they magically know where to go
because that is what they were perfectly created to do?

When the birds reach the other side,
do they fall on their knees and kiss the ground?
do they stop for a moment and sing,
perhaps strut their colors, give thanks?

. . .

. . .

It's good the sky can't be fenced
(though I suspect we are trying).
It's good that passports and borders are earthbound
otherwise the man behind the desk at the port of entry
might ask
Do you have a license for that craft?
A visa?
How long do you plan to stay?
Do you have a plan?

# IN THE LABRADOR TEA

Along the abandoned railroad track
we were gazing at the Labrador tea,
their flowers sprinkled white in the bog,
when a sandhill crane materialized
from the sphagnum ooze.

And then just in front of it.
another stood up.

And once we got our breath back,
we started smiling at our blindness,
our good fortune,
their grace.

Then one of them stepped away
while the other paced in a small circle.
We realized then
she had been sitting on a nest.

We watched for a moment only,
knowing that to honor her,
we had to walk on.

When we looked back,
she was incubating her eggs,
eggs that housed thousands of years of DNA,
the evolved summation of all cranes.

Earlier that day, we had watched two cranes
sailing over a nearby marsh
like Spanish galleons.

. . .

. . .

They never flapped their wings
until they lowered their spindly legs
landed with a short trot
closed their wings.
Then they paused,
bowed to one another,
opened their wings,
leapt up in the air once,
twice,
folded their wings

and gazed down.

# EBONY JEWELWINGS

A bog is an odd place to write a history book.
It's dark and oozy in the peat,
but perhaps this is how all history emerges.

I leave the pollen analysis to the scientists
who have to strain over microscopes
while I watch the ebony jewelwing damselflies dance,
smell the exquisite perfume of the horned bladderwort,
poke around for dying insects in the flared vases of pitcher plants,
and bounce on the bog mat like a child on a trampoline
while the cold water creeps into my shoes.

In Europe, they've pulled two-thousand-year-old people out of bogs
with the nooses still around their necks,
their bodies bronzed in the bog tannins.
They were flung there in dishonor,
the manicured grass burial grounds unfit for their kind.

But I like the quiet here,
the small wildness.

Perhaps it was more of an honor than they supposed
to be tossed aside,
to settle slowly among the many lives
that have had to struggle so long
in the cold moss.

To sleep among the orchids, the cottongrass,
all the anonymous sedges,
maybe to arise again two thousand years hence
among the clamoring scientists
amidst the wild peace that will still be
in the hovering hum,
together with the ebony jewelwings,
perhaps that would be a grace after all.

# *THIS STILL NIGHT*

*Let the beauty we love be what we do.*
*There are hundreds of ways to kneel and kiss the ground.*
– Rumi

On this still night, the stars
reflect from the black water,
blending the horizon between sky and lake
so that I'm a little dizzy
a little unsure of where I am

until a lost breath of wind ripples the water
and my canoe rocks for a moment
reminding me of the tremors in my life
which are no more than this,
this holiness,
briefly stirred,
only briefly stirred,
this
holiness.

# TANGLED

In the cedar swamp,
the fallen simply won't die.
Instead, they grow upright from their branches.
One tree turns into a dozen.
But eventually a wind rises
and those fall too,
and then their branches grow up into new trees
each a dozen or more again.

Until the swamp becomes all arms
hugging one another (if you bring some light)
or choking one another (if you bring some dark)
an ensnarement,
a tree web.

They grow very old.
Perhaps for a millennia or more
they embrace.

The cedars become a place for imagination,
for fear
or magic
as life is always the story we wish to tell that day.

When I am among them
I talk,
envisioning my family branches,
all too old to unsnarl
but which still form the living tissue
within which I breathe.
I'm like the black muck beneath my feet,
full of forgotten lives,
swallowed in the tide of needles and trunks
that have drifted down
or keeled over.

But here I am despite all that,
because of all that.
So I smear the mud in my hands,
give thanks,
then pick my way back out

into the light.

# PILGRIMAGE

*Let us bless the humility of water,*
*Always willing to take the shape*
*Of whatever otherness holds it.*
– John O'Donahue

That this water has emerged from this ground
to bring forth these lives –
the bluegill, the loon
the mussel, the lily
the otter, the dragonfly –
is a grace I surely don't deserve
but which I am doing all I know
to embrace.

The water moves in pilgrimage
always kneeling on lower ground
sinuous in its grace
every wave another lapped meaning
on its shores
coming again
again
in case we forget
where we began
what we are made of
where we are going.

woods

# FIRST SNOW

I don't know whether to be quiet or jubilant.
The first snow of November
has turned every tree branch white.

Should I meditate on the beauty
or make dozens of snow angels?

I stand undecided,
hands on hips,
smiling.

Of course, it matters not one whit what I do.
All that matters is that my heart is open
that the beauty rushes in
that I respond with joy,
a joy which doesn't care about form.
I can pray joyfully
or run joyfully dumping snow from laden limbs.

It's all the same.
All reverence
All innocence
All thankfulness
All grace.

# AFTER THE STORM

After the storm,
random chaos reigns,
or so it appears,
the big trees all laid down
into jackstraws.

The heart hurts
to see so much beauty,
beauty that we knew wasn't eternal
but spoke of the eternal,
to see all of that torn apart
in what seems senseless, brutal, perhaps shameful.

What we don't know is that this same woods,
the one we walked in so silently yesterday before the storm,
sprang from just such a downburst four centuries ago,
followed by drought and a seering fire,
an apparent cremation of all that mattered.

And then the disorder began to order.
The loss became gain.
The death became healing.
That was this woods before the wind's blast,
where we sat with our backs
against the giant pines and hemlocks,
eyes falling closed to let the real world seep in
through our skin,
our breath.

Does the forest mourn its loss?
Or has its language failed to conceive the word,
instead investing in change,
in resilience,
in the myriad fungi and invertebrates
who understand
how a community lives
over time
and for one another.

# BURNING COLD

Forty below at first light.
The old house popped all night,
wooden bones snapping
in a thundering of icy expansions.

In the woods, the cells in the trees burst.
It sounded like sporadic gunfire,
a running sniper battle.

That is, until the sun crested the hills.

Then the air glittered with phantasmic particles.
And though the sun's rays felt lifeless,
the world began to warm
and the firefight calmed.

I walked outside
(even the snow cracked)
and my cheeks immediately burned.
Even my eyes burned.
I took off my gloves to fill the bird feeder
and the infinitely cold metal scorched my fingers.

I closed my eyes, faced the sun,
and scarlet suffused behind my eyes
another burning.

I reminded myself that I must sit more in the sun
not let the cold burn me
not let it turn me into brittle shards
that explode in small gasps at night.

It's so easy to get lost.

The birds are shivering,
I'm shivering,
my muscles contracting to generate heat
luscious, calming heat
to save me from all this burning.

# HOW TO ENTER A WOODS

The parking lot tells the first story:
how fast the cars roar into the lot.
are the radios cranked?
are the doors slammed?
do the voices emerge like party goers?
do they line up to be sprayed with mosquito dope?
are they raring to GO, doing stretches, bouncing up and down?

Everyone arrives with a suitcase.

No matter.
Here's what matters:

They are here.

However loud, however brash, however inattentive,
they are here to walk into the woods.

I have faith that the woods will do its work in its quiet way.

It takes time to slough off the job, the boss,
the traffic,
Fox news,
bear fears, wolf fears, tick fears.
everything in the suitcase they've been dragging around for years
and are still filling up.

The trees and birds and wildflowers will try to empty it
and then refill it with
some seeds
a clump of damp moss
some bright tiny mushrooms
a handful of berries,
then more seeds.
And eventually time will blend it
to be poured into their open, cupped hands,

and they will drink.

# EPHEMERALS

When the spring winds come,
it is easy to believe in God.
The resurrection blooms
outside every church door
in arbutus white
hepatica purple.

The sun ministers first to the south-facing hillsides
while the sinners on the north-face
must wait their grace.
But they too will receive the call,
each in their own time.

Unlike us,
most flowers open at their appointed moment,
not cursed with free will
to believe or not believe
in the sun
the rain
the warming dirt.

# FIRST FROST

Late August and it's 27° this morning.
In the wetlands below our house,
the sedges shine white in the rosy sunrise.
In the garden, the tomatoes have failed to follow
the first commandment of autumn:
Thou Shall Not Freeze.
Unpicked tomatoes hang on limp branches,
each stem like Atlas crumpled
beneath the Earth he once bore.

The rising sun quickly changes the predawn frost
into droplets as simple as gentle rain,
except frost kills unmercifully,
a magic moment reached when cells burst without a cry,
ice expanding within,
cutting cell walls like a balloon punctured
after a long birthday party.

Frost is like a quick tear in a fabric,
a renting weakness that will tear further
nearly every morning over the next eight months
until the rescue of May.

Insects better have laid eggs by now,
trusting everything to a new generation.
The insect-eating birds better have left, too,
this momentary white slate,
this foreshadow of winter.

And the mammals better be weaving their new coats
cause it's coming.
That long slow train will stall and exhale
its engine breath,
a cold steam that will turn a once lush sea of green
into an undulation of white

and the rich soundful joy
that marked spring as the great resurrector
will mute like a trumpet bell
stuffed with white cloth.

The quiet time is coming.
Get ready.

# ALIGHT

Minus ten degrees this morning.
We break trail on wooden skis,
struggling around fallen aspens,
the splayed and broken white birch.
In the understory, the whip-like stems of hazelnut
tangle in our hair.

A half-mile in, we come to a living wall,
ancient hemlock, sugar maple, yellow birch,
forty acres risen
from the surrounding clearcut sea
where the youthful aspen stand shoulder to shoulder
like corn in a winter field,
each aspen racing to the sun
because there's death in the shadows,
panic, too
like people feel when a fire breaks out
and there's only one exit.

We step from their clutch
into the ancient grove.
Here randomly
some have fallen
and flowered with moss.

This forest knows centuries of dalliances,
loves,
hunts,
deaths.

The dark hemlocks speak solemnly –
quiet down, look in, fill up, they say.
And though I'm never sure how to pray,
or why we think every thought isn't a prayer already,
I pray.

The only answer
is the simple music of a black-capped chickadee,
its song adrift
alight
in the hemlock dark.

# THE MOSSES

The voices retune
when I close my eyes
when I follow my breath
when I say thank you
when I place my fingertips together
to be a small basket to fill.

Then the hemlocks nod further,
the cedars bow lower,
and in ebbs grace,
a bit like the mosses opening to the mist
that is everywhere and nowhere,
the mist that now reforms into droplets,
into something that would seem too soft to hear,
but which I realize is the percussion of this forest
the beat that lulls me,
nets me,
until I come back
- not awaken -
but come back
after being absorbed
like the mist by the mosses who,
and I mean who,
ask for so little.

Calm comes in the voice
of waves on the sand
covering
uncovering.

In wind through needles
translating
humming.

By stones rubbing in water's
inwash
outwash.

By sunlight on soil
receiving
radiating.

...

. . .

And by the mosses
who transform all edges
into roundness
into what feels like kindness,
into where we become the same kind,
the same kin.

# HOW OLD IS THIS WOODS?

The lady asks me, "How old is this woods?"

I proceed to list facts and figures:
The maximum ages of these tree species,
the average ages of these other species,
how long a species can live in the shade of its elders,
how many seeds this one produces ever year,
how many may germinate,
how many deer likely winter here and browse the buds,
what this fire scar means,
how old these mossy logs might be,
how long ago that stump might have been a tree,
what the Ojibwe might have been gathering here, or hunting, or cutting,
why this particular area has small trees and that one giants,
why this tree has low branches and this one no branches for 60 feet,
how many generations of tree have probably come and gone  . . .

And now the woman clearly wishes she never asked the question.

But there's the problem –
quick answers are for simple problems,
and there's nothing simple about an old forest.
Lives and deaths mix by the minute, hour, day, month, year, decade,
century . . .
and one can't find the end of the string and say this is the beginning
any more than one can find the other end and say this is the end.

Age is just a number,
people say with a smile to old folks.

Right.

The woods are very old and very young.

That is my answer.

# WHEN THE BLUE JAY SINGS

When the blue jay sings,
his whole body bobs up and down
as if giving voice required the sum of his being.

When the song sparrow sings,
he throws back his head delivering an oratory
as if to make the clouds part.

When the winter wren sings,
he jumbles a hundred notes together
as if it might be his last joy.

And when the hermit thrush sings,
he harmonizes with himself
as if to say, yes,
you can live in two worlds.

When I sing,
I notice I always smile.
I'm not establishing a territory,
or wooing a mate.
I'm singing because some kindness
has risen in me,
some instinct to be music
such that I'm dreaming to be a bird on a branch
with the newborn sun in my eyes,
the long slants of light
soft on the mossy logs that hold the rain,
the wood decaying in a music of its own.

In fact, there are times when everything
is singing
through the open door of my heart.
And just for a moment I can hear it all
as the moss must hear it, too.
And there's no breath.
Just sun, just song.

# MEANING TO STAY

(from a line in Wendell Berry's poem "2010 XI," in *This Day*)

Come, meaning to stay.
For what is home
if you aren't meant to be there?
If you aren't always grateful, giddy even, to return?
If the returning isn't as joyous as the departures to whatever
paradise?

The river is always home
despite its endless departures.
Within its banks
over its banks
a trickle or a torrent
it comes, stays, leaves,
is past, present, future,
like the breath.

Invest all of who you are in a place
and then you may call it a home.
You may come home,
be home.

An admonition – don't confuse a house with a home.
It's the soil, the smell
of a garden planted
a field plowed or mowed,
the autumn leaves on the woods trail,
the mud on the river bank
where the otter eats his crayfish and laughs,
then slides back into his home.

It's the trees you planted,
the summer fruits,
the birds who call your home home
and sing it back into riches every May.
Count the birds as your stock portfolio
and balance your books everyday with walks
into your still wild home
into your still wild heart
where you come every day to stay.

# TRAPPING BEARS

A friend of mine catches bears
in barrel traps baited
with candy bars.
He's caught a female today
that was content in a corn field.
He drugs her
and hangs her up in a white pine
like summer laundry
though the wind doesn't starch her
doesn't breathe the North into her.
She hangs collapsed like my tomatoes
after the first freeze.

My friend weighs her
takes out a tooth
measures her paws, her length
lectures me on her life cycle
and gives me a claw that has broken off.
Then he lowers her down gently
from wind to grass
and we winch her back into the barrel.

She smells.
Insects mob her.
Her tongue droops to the side.

I'd asked to see this
but I'm not sure now.

Later we release her across river.
She runs briefly into the woods
and then deftly scales high up a red pine.
She's back in the world again
a massive bird on a limb
snapping her teeth at us
like the closing of a steel trap.

# OPENING DAY

Deer season opened today.

In our garden, deer eat our apple trees, our elderberries, our plum trees.

In the woods, the deer
eat the white cedar, the hemlock, the Canada yew, the sugar maple.
Five pounds of browse every winter day
a thousand buds, give or take.

Some say there are too many of them.
Kill as many as we can they say
and then hope
that a cruel winter takes most of the rest!

Others think of their beauty, their grace,
their astonishing speed.

I once watched one jump over a small spruce
and hang in the air for a moment like a Christmas ornament.

I admire their guile,
their fearlessness through winter nights
when coyotes and wolves circle.

I try to breathe through their flaring nostrils
and feel the fear of Opening Day when death rains.

Everyday I also see the deaths of the car-shattered deer
twisted in a blood pool beside the road.

I have seen death enough not to wish it on anything.

Opening Day makes me think a lot about death,
yours and mine and all the others.

I think, too, of my apple trees
their pink-white blossoms,
formed from spring buds the deer didn't get,
perfect and sweet in May
when everyday is also
Opening Day.

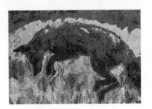

# RED FOX

By 5:10 the sky had awakened
in a soft peach and blue
and the red fox was trotting
down the double yellow center line
across the bridge that spanned the river
the river that was seeping fog
into the green-graced marsh.
The song sparrow was singing from the willows,
as was the yellow warbler,
and so, too, the red-eyed vireo
high in the black ash
who too often forgets that a little silence
would make his song more beautiful.

Venus was still burning in the East
right over the spot where the sun would rise
and in my scope I could see three of Jupiter's moons
lined up perfectly like an arrow shot.

Oh, and the robins were caroling all around
such pleasure they take in the first light,
and a crane bugled from somewhere down the river
and the red-winged blackbirds "oak-a-leed" again and again
while the young eagle leaned
over the edge of its immense nest
crying and crying for its breakfast to be dropped
cold and wet at its feet

When I noticed the fox
was crouched in the gravel
at the end of the bridge
watching.

Then some spark lit in its eye
and it ran like a red dart
into the long grasses of the marsh
and was
gone.

# THE GREAT GRAYS
## SAILED OUT

The great grays sailed out of Canada
hungry, silent, elegant,
stalking lumberyards, parking lots, airports, roadsides.
One sat for days on a windowsill at a local McDonalds
patient for the spilled french fry
that would entice a neighborhood mouse.
Another perched on a stop sign
along a Minnesota farm road
amidst a bleakness,
scanning a flat horizon and fields of snow.

We pulled up, rolled down the window,
said "Good afternoon! Welcome!"
He, or she, blinked a yellow eye
as impassive as the flat white all around us.

We took a photo.

The winds were skittering snow devils,
18 degrees on the car thermometer.
The stop sign offered elevation over the corn stubble
that fed pockets of mice,
whole communities under the snow
who wouldn't know
who couldn't imagine
what would explode their subnivean world,
clutching them,
lifting them,
dangling them
in a gray sky
under gray wings beating, beating,
and finally folding on a tiny hillock of snow,
into a cottage of warmth.

And then all dark,
a death that was illumined by a last minute of life,
by a flight into a wind,
into a landscape of light,
and held in an embrace,
excited, curious.

# SMALL THINGS

I have been spending my life
accumulating many small things.

In late April, I find trailing arbutus in flower
under the ridged old white pines.

In early May, I discover the first hermit thrush
singing within the hemlocks
its spiraling opera.

Every day, new things arrive,
or bloom, or are born, or die,
and I try to find as many of them as I can.

I don't collect them in plastic bags,
or put them in vases,
or pin them on cardboard,
or exile them to my freezer,

or eat them.

I just try to find them.

I find them sometimes with my ears,
sometimes by nearly stepping on them,
sometimes they just come to me
when I am sitting.

If I were to put them all in a container,
they would look like nothing more than where I am now
which is laying under a white pine
that is leaning over the river
a river flowing so softly I can only hear it
now and again
amidst the birds that sing
among the needles that fall.

# NO REASON

*And*
*For no reason*
*I start skipping like a child.*
*And*
*For no reason*
*I turn into a leaf*
*That is carried so high*
*I kiss the Sun's mouth*
*And dissolve.*
*And*
*For no reason*
*A thousand birds*
*Choose my head for a conference table,*
*Start passing their*
*Cups of wine*
*And their wild songbooks all around.*

So wrote Hafiz.

What reason do you think you need?
There is only this beauty
There is only this joy
There is only this life.

How will you choose to honor it?
What prayer would mean all that you want to say?
What gesture could show God how thankful you are?

Do you need a reason to be the violin
that sings life awake?
Do you need a reason to love anything?

Reasons are a tepid water.
We didn't come into this world on thoughtful reason
but on the breath of passion
where nothing mattered except that moment.

That is the reason to be alive,
to love this moment
as your first and last breath.

And then, like Hafiz, to start skipping.

# GHOSTS

*(upon reading an article projecting
the loss of millions of species due to climate change)*

Many ghosts already roam this land.
The Passenger Pigeon,
the Carolina Parakeet,
the Heath Hen.

Some species are ghosts in waiting,
alive but already splintered
into ragtag remnants hiding
along the edge,
hanging on in tiny encampments.

Wrote Rainer Maria Rilke,
*Perhaps we are only here for saying:*
*House, Bridge, Fountain, Gate . . .*
*But to say them . . .*
*oh, to say them*
*more intensely than the Things themselves ever dreamed of being.*

In Europe I could say
Azure-winged Magpie.
In Australia I could say
Boyd's Forest Dragon.

But I live here,
the Northwoods of Wisconsin.

So I say
Pine, Spruce, Cedar, Hemlock
Loon, Winter Wren, Blackburnian Warbler
Gray Wolf, Moose, Snowshoe Hare
Mink Frog, Brook Trout
Red-backed Salamander
Spring Azure Butterfly
Labrador Tea, Cranberry
Dragon's Mouth Orchid

. . .

...

I am trying at this particular moment
to say White-throated Sparrow.
White-Throated Sparrow.
White-throated sparrow.

I'm talking about this white-throated sparrow,
the one singing from the river edge
as the night succumbs to grey dawn.

I want to talk with birds.
I mean TALK.
I want to know everything.

Right now, I want to know why this white-throated sparrow sings
with such silver clarity
while the alder flycatcher has so plainly little to say.

And how is it that its song says NORTH?
That when I hear the white-throat
(Oh, sweet Canada Canada Canada)
I see the crimson-pink flower of bog laurel
smell sphagnum moss
feel the soft threads of cottongrass between my fingers?

To speak of this tiny bird as Rilke asks of me,
I must hear its Otherness,
I must know how to sing in celebration of a long night gone by,
I must know how to grace the wind with an ecstatic simplicity
that says
White-throated Sparrow.

I kneel in prayer.
I dance,
dancing with the ghosts,
dancing with the living,
dancing with the dying.

The light and the shadow are in the trees
on the water
among the rocks.

# THE OLDEST LIVING THING

The oldest living thing I know may be this hemlock
or perhaps this pine or sugar maple or yellow birch.

So what? some have asked.

Think of Copernicus or Galileo,
of Magellan or Geronimo,
of DNA,
of love,
of beauty.

Think of the rocks on this esker
that were carried in the icy tumult
then dropped unceremoniously,
the ceremony now conducted
in the attention I offer them
among the soft mosses.

Think of the music on the wind
how it feels old, too,
something about how far the wind had to travel
to be interpreted by these needles and leaves,
and sung into existence.

I am listening,
realizing I'm holding my breath
my eyes gazing now at every little thing
and then the smaller things all around them.

Oh, the world is stunning
if you lose consciousness
fall out of time
and find the place where you belong,
breathing in centuries of others belonging.

Revel in the sap being cooked.
Revel in the steaming breath of a red fox
walking the fallen hemlock
above the smothering snow.
Watch him sniff the air.
Watch him unearth the wildness
this place offers.

# WINTER WREN SINGS

When the winter wren sings
the notes make a riot in the leaves
as if the wind rose from every direction
and blew and blew
for seven seconds
then stopped,
reminding us
why we fell in love
with the world.

When the winter wren sings
he invites us to join
his whirling dervish dance
a dizzying and heartbursting dance
a time when shafts of light sweeten the air,
the air that we breathe
when we finally remember to breathe.

When the winter wren sings
children stop chasing
and cock their heads
listening to his ecstasy
that takes them as far as their imaginations can go,
a voice that makes them fall
onto the wild ground
to lay among the cushions of mosses
and to laugh
in the dirt.

# TO WALK IN RADIANCE

(a phrase from Wendell Berry in *This Day,* "1986 – 1")

The common sunlight
translated through millions of needles
sifts into shafts,
into ribs of radiance
poured through the hemlocks,
a phantasmagoria of winking rivulets
like a million fireflies blinking in the bottomlands.

To walk within such radiance,
to sit among the radiance,
to close and open one's eyes and behold this radiance,
perhaps I have awakened at last into my prayers,
or entered the prayers of these hemlocks.

This morning they have found themselves
in the midst of a benediction
one that their age has earned.
The intricacies of the needles have puzzled
this together over centuries,
the particles in the air suspended
without a breath of wind
inexplicably and clearly
holy.

Perhaps, this is the breath of hemlocks
made incandescently soft and silent.

I'm silent, too.
I have wished to be just this -
the absolute silence pierced by light made visible.

# NINETY DEGREES

The forecast calls for 90° today,
so I'm out early to enjoy the morning coolness and the slanted light.
The world is already starting to busy,
trucks rumbling by,
competing with the sweet songs of rose-breasted grosbeaks
and American redstarts whose particular song this morning
sounds like someone shaking castanets.

The male lands close to me,
all black and orange like a Halloween trick-or-treater.
Then a black-billed cuckoo starts up in the distance,
a hollow "coo-coo-coo, coo-coo-coo, coo-coo-coo,"
and soon a song sparrow spills his jumbling song.

And then I notice the wind has come up
and the willows in the wetland below are waving as if they were fluid,
and the silver maples, though stiffer,
still do a doe-see-doe
with the can't-make-up-its-mind breeze.

And now the sun has disappeared behind a bank of clouds
and there's a momentary chill.
I wonder if the red-eyed vireo,
who has never stopped singing this whole time
notes these things, too,
or just lives wholly present in his song,
all the rest just noise to him.
It must be hard to notice other things
when you're singing the same chorus
22,176 times a day.
So counted John Burroughs
who took the time to keep track from dawn to dusk,
though I wonder how he kept his attention on the vireo
when the rest of the world around him was surely singing, too.

Burroughs must have had to fight,
fiercely so,
all the other temptations of the day,
because each life beckons so richly,
each a branch the mind flits to
and perches for a moment,
alive in that momentary stream of sun,
listening to each perfect song.

# RESILIENCE

The snow kept falling,
first all night,
then all the next day,
squalling and quieting,
then squalling again,
the pines across the river appearing and disappearing
like a bobber on a lake
their flagged tops
sometimes floating in the sky
like disembodied green gods
surveying the soft deluge.

Then the startling sky materialized.
A blue spotlight first,
and then a blue sea.
The slanting sun draped
the slumped spruces and firs
once so elegant, so graceful,
but now bowed in seeming prayer,
each branch supported by the one below
in a monkey pile of wood and snow and needles.

Perhaps the supple wood was silently groaning
under the immense weight.
But I think it was smiling,
awaiting the moment when the snow would finally slide off
and the branches spring up
waving to the world a hello again,
nodding to the sky that you couldn't break us,
we're still here
in your sun
in this soil
open-armed
ready to receive,
ready to give.

# TREE MATH

Predawn,
the time when it's light enough to just see forms of trees.

And I'm doing math.

Let's see: 600 years-old x 365 days = 219,000.
That's 219,000 chances for a western red cedar
to feel the dark surrender to the light.
Not far south, coastal redwoods get 730,000 such resurrections
(2,000 years x 365 days)
though for both cedars and redwoods,
the glory of sunrise is often little more than the subtlety
between black rainfog and gray rainfog,
a study perfect for charcoal artists.

I'm also thinking about the math of plumbing:
250 feet into the mist for the terminal bud of the cedar,
360 feet lost in the fog for the redwood.
Each requires discourse and trade far below
with roots and mycelium,
all translating dirt, wind, and light,
feats so slowly performed in their tent show of abracadabras
that we miss them no matter our mindfulness.

The plumbing, though, that's the final arbiter,
the crucial architectural design required to pump sap to the tip top,
which,
and you're welcome to try this by hand in your own home,
is hard to do with no mechanical parts and no fossil fuels.

It's more than plumbing though.
The ghostly white mycelium,
the threadlike roots of fungi,
snake everywhere underground,
casting a net through the soil
seining for water and nutrients,
connecting this tree to that tree
to that tree to that tree
everyone holding hands in a vast underground internet of tree talk,
trading goods and services without Dow or Jones complicating things.

. . .

...

Meanwhile, at the top of the tree, wind flows by for centuries
carrying dust and seeds and leaves that collect in the branches,
growing forest gardens
of huckleberries, elderberries, gooseberries, ferns.

Why are we here? What is asked of us? How do we reciprocate?
Perhaps it is as simple as putting our faith in loving
this most inconceivable place,
in walking in everyone's shoes –
fungi, lichens, mosses, soil, fog, light –
and letting that wandering love guide us
to the top of a tree
into the fungal mats
into the light and mist.

# DESCENTS ASCENTS

It's starting to rain,
or perhaps the aspen leaves are just dancing in the wind,
this dusk when the veery is singing
its notes spiraling
down
down
down
a song of falling leaves
a song of hearts finally calm.

The song is joined by the hermit thrush
whose notes climb to heaven
up
up
up.

I stand utterly still
and watch
as the coming dark
and the moonlight
pool and sift
between the charcoal tree trunks.

I wish I could forget
this body I came in.
I wish I was this moonlit rain
dappling its kindness,
its chant
onto the leaves.

## WIND IN PINES

The ancient white pine
seems to ask me
to sit by it.
So I lean my back against its
sculpted rough ridges
and find the place
where my skeleton fits.
Then I have nothing to do
but watch and listen.

A pine warbler trills loosely,
then a blue-headed vireo adds its sweetness.

And the wind begins to move,
sifting
humming
ssshhhhing
through the pine's needles.

The wind would have no voice
without these hands to interpret it.

What better translation could there be
than the soft fingers
of waxy needles rubbing against one another
like the combing of hair
like water washing through sand
like a mother soothing her child.

# THE ORIGINAL FACE

The original face of this landscape had no face.
It had moods and lightings
endless winters
jubilant springs
tumultuous storms
peace
deaths
glory and gore and praise.

No flash represents the multitude.
This original changeling
never stood still for a photo.

But there is an original essence
an original feeling
that embraced all the faces
held all the breath
resonated a sound
still in our blood.
It trembles there,
then flows forth
in an original, soft,
whisper.

Once, I thought I heard it.
I laid down in the mosses
next to a hermit thrush nest
with its broken green-blue eggs.
Then I heard the male thrush singing.
Up to heaven he went every time
and I along with him
praising and thanking
the very air,
which didn't care one way or another,
but never stopped
shimmering.

# WOLF'S MILK SLIME

We look for mushrooms in the silence
of an August deep woods,
when even the mosquitoes no longer sing.

The rains fell hard and often this summer,
so the moistness said,
Let there be mushrooms!
and the multitudes rose,
a prodigal forthcoming of hues,
brilliant red parasols and flat egg-yolk dance floors
perfect for late night chipmunk revelry.

We delight in finding the odd things –
the wolf milk's slime that we pop with a stick
so they ooze pink,
the orange jelly that exudes
from fissures in long-dead wood,
the dead man's fingers and the black trumpets
which lend a funereal note to the gaiety
as do the other fungi that have gone by and are rotting,
a misery of forms that we poke
and go "Ooooo!"
then laugh like junior high kids.

The forests are now a shambling celebration of the end game.
The engine of summer sputters,
the air nips,
and a singular bright energy emerges
that the humid summer had slowly dripped away.

"That's all she wrote," my father would say.
Yes, this year's novel has reached a climax
but with plot twists still to come.
And the main characters?
Rotters, all of them,
to the core.

HOME

# OPENING THE DOOR

How do we open the door to compassion?

"What good are sturgeon?" a man asked in a meeting.
"I don't eat them.
I say get rid of them."

Another time, another meeting,
a fellow shouted, "What good are wolves?
All they do is eat our deer.
I say kill them all!"

Once, even, a guy said to me,
"What good are loons?
They eat all the fish!"
He, of course,
thought the only good one was a dead one.

I want to say,
"What good, then, are you?"
"What good are your children?"

I remember this as I stand next to a black spruce
in a bog close to our home.
The spruce is a scraggly thing,
mostly just a tuft of growth at the top,
skinny,
probably very old.

It's small.

At its feet are bog laurel and bog rosemary
growing out of a bed of sphagnum moss.
The tiny leaves of bog cranberry
weave themselves around their base.
They, too, are very small.

The laurel is in flower.
I can't describe for you how beautiful it is.
What need is there for words
when your heart is so open?

# SECOND SKIN

We lay in bed at dawn and listen.
It's late August
a Sunday morning.
The windows are open
a cool breeze skims over the bed.
A lone crow calls insistently
while a juvenile eagle in the nest across the river
cries for food.

Mary is curled on her side.
I wrap myself around her
like a second skin
like the peel on a slice of orange.

I fit tight to her and breathe
in rhythm with her
expanding
contracting
as if my lungs were hers.
I lightly rub her shoulder
and she gets goose bumps.

I like to lay my hand in the coil of her hip
or gently cradle the curve under one of her breasts.

This is joy.
This is what marriage should be.
Peel me away
you find her
peel her away
you find me.

# DELICIOUS

I like the word delicious
It's so open to possibility.
The tea I drink, yes, but
the grackle's unrepentant disharmony – delicious
the dangling fluttering aspen flowers – delicious
the decay in the rising marsh air – delicious
the slow fuse of the wood fire – delicious
the robin's frenetic greeting of dawn – delicious
the cool warmth of Mary's skin – delicious
just the way the word sounds in my mouth . . .
delicious.

In growing older, we need to unlearn so many things
one of which is to recall how to run down the path
to the next thing
and then to taste it
not swirling it around like some sophisticate's pretentious wine
but to mouth it up exultantly.

For everything in this most imaginative of worlds
requires an exuberant tasting
just for the chance of it,
and whether bitter or sweet
reminds us,
right now,
we're alive.

# HER FINGER TO HER LIPS

When I was a young child and sick,
my mother would put her finger to her lips
and sssshhhh me,
healing my discomfort,
my fear,
until I slept

just as the wind in the pines
sssshhhh
heals me
sssshhhh
and leads me to sleep.

Later I open my eyes
brain muddled
but so quiet.

And then the gratitude
floods in,
along with the smells of the damp leaves
and the deepest green,
my body now so relaxed
that I'm not sure I'm still in it.

Such is peace
that I wonder if I'm the flat stone I'm sitting on.

I touch a leaf
surprised that my finger doesn't flow through it.

# WADING

I like footbridges,
all kinds,
over rivers and brooks,
over chasms and train tracks,
over little roads.

I like to feel how my heart
can cross each one in a different way
ending up on some other side
transformed.

I also like the feel of handrails.
I made one once
for my elderly father-in-law
who when he visited
used it to pull himself up three stairs,
and when he left for his home,
used it to steady himself on the trek back down.

He lived upstream
on the same river as the one we live on,
where at 95,
he crossed his final bridge.
Cane in hand,
I wonder what he held on to?
Or did he run on youthful legs?

Every so often I think I see him
on the other side,
wading in the water,
pointing down the river with his cane,
laughing.

# SEND OWNER'S MANUAL

I'd like to receive the owner's manual to this body I was given.
Someone must have it and is enjoying taunting me.

For that matter, I'd like the owner's manual we should have
received to this Earth.
I imagine it would be part assembly
part maintenance
part manifesto.

I have questions.

At what point do our cells stop growing and start aging?
I want to see the schematic on that.

I'd like to see the blueprint on our brain.
It doesn't seem to work like an engine or an appliance.
Why does it perform so differently one day to the next?

And Annie died young from cancer
which made no sense because she was so young,
so healthy
and she loved children.
Are there diagrams to explain this?

I think the manual should have a rulebook, too,
otherwise it's like we were spun on a roulette wheel
which I don't see so much as unfair
as just odd,
and not very thoughtful.

Well, my model is a 1951, white, genetic mutt
with no cultural roots left anywhere
and thus roots everywhere.
If you've seen the manual
send it soon.

# RIPENING

Now the quiet at dawn has grown nearly complete
except for the aspen leaves
sifting the wind like soft rain.
A red-eyed vireo starts up and sings and sings
unwilling to let go of the primal spring
that all the rest, in their silence,
have agreed was enough.

The cool air hangs damp
against the just bluing sky
while the quarter moon burns
not setting
but just fading
into a brighter whole.
Occasionally a mourning dove exhales its melancholy.
And now and again different birds fly by
or land close, each sounding of their wingbeats
a surprising flutter.

Late July and the summer has peaked.
I can feel a transformation
another round of exuberance coming
but with an undertone spoken
by the mourning of the doves
who are saying *It's gone, gone, gone.*

A long slanting light illuminates the tops of the highest pines.
Perhaps the doves are also saying,
*Morning, it's here, here, here.*

Inside is homemade bread
blueberry jam we made last week
strawberry jam we made three weeks earlier.
The elderberries and grapes are darkening,
the blackberries and thimbleberries still to come.

The birds have sung these berries ripe.

The waxwings and robins and veeries take their share now
their fat chicks crying their pleasure because
it's late July
and the world is full.

# DAZZLE

The ruby-throated hummingbird
keeps buzzing into the feeder
all dark in the shadows of the young morning
a silhouette awaiting that first shaft of light.

I suppose I am, too,
though I don't wish to only reflect the light
no matter the stunning dazzle.
I don't want the light to come and go
depending on how I turn my head.
black to scarlet to coal to fire.

There he is again, sipping the sugar water.
I wish I could make a wild nectar
of beebalm, jewelweed, columbine
a little funnel of all that is sweet
all that is the alchemy of light and rain and soil.

There are holy wells in Ireland
but perhaps these are just as holy
that a hummingbird may drink from them,
hovering in the light,
and dazzling the sun.

# ALLY ALLY IN FREE

Standing under the streetlight,
a child,
the shadows long, forbidding,
giving up,
I'd call, "Ally ally in free."
"Ally ally in free."

And slowly my friends would slip
laughing from the shadows.

"Where were you?"

"I'm not telling!"
they would smile.

When it was my turn to hide
I wouldn't tell either,
except sometimes when no matter how hard they tried,
they couldn't find me.
Then the fun went out of it,
and I'd tell.

Because where is the joy if you can't be found?

"Come out, come out, wherever you are!"

In prayer this morning
I asked the Divine to come out
and I asked my Spirit to come out,
both hiding
as they like to
in the shadows.

And like standing under that streetlight
looking for my childhood friends,
I knew they were near.

Ally ally in free.
Ally ally in free.

# STEPPING ACROSS A BORDER

I don't expect everyone to understand
what border I step across
when I push off into the river
or when I enter an ancient woods.
We all ring ourselves within undrawn lines
hiring guards only we can see
demanding papers
we were never given.

So, we turn back.
Or even if we cross,
we were never really there,
blindfolded by our fears,
the mind firing like hot oil on water.

If I write of wind in a pine
and your mind is in a traffic jam,
what chance do my words have?
If I ask you to smell the first trailing arbutus of spring
and you've never been on your knees
in a pine woods
after a hard winter,
will you read on?
If my words ask you to breathe in a fog over a wild lake
and your breath is running somewhere else
with so much to do,
where will we meet?
I am lost to you
as you are to me.

Come cross the border.

# STOKING THE FIRE

Waking, I come down to stoke the fire
now gone to coal and ash after the long night.
The house pops, sudden shots of contracting wood.
I open the door to listen for owls,
but nothing.
Minus 20 the thermometer claims.

I think the silence of deep cold
surpasses the silence of warmth.
There's less promise, more regret,
a withdrawing.

Dry cedar sparks the fire and now it is popping, too.
Outside contracting, inside expanding.
The stove joins in, steadily ticking,
the warming metal sides chanting their pleasure of
blessed heat, blessed heat, blessed heat.

I pull up a rocking chair, close,
but first stand with my back to the stove
until my pants and shirt grow hot,
and then I sit.

The fire offers light
enough to read or write by
if I angle the paper just right.

The water on the stove starts to simmer,
and the morning choir becomes pop, click, simmer,
plus the creak of the rocking chair.

It's an odd music,
metal and wood and water talking in this way,
but the old sounds help to open pathways,
an idea comes unanticipated,
and then the pen begins its work.

## *HOT CHOCOLATE*

All day the snow fell and fell.

The silence grew apace,
ever softer.

And soon everything seemed wrapped in a grandmother's shawl,
all the edges gone.

Some silences are hard.
They ache or slice or bite.
They make you smaller.

But the silence of this ever-snowing . . .
the big flakes,
heavy with their gentle purpose,
gather into an unwoven blanket
made of calm.

All one can do is watch,
breathe in the rhythm,
dream,
remember,
fall in love again,

and drink hot chocolate.

# WHEN MARY SITS AT HER LOOM

When Mary sits at her loom
and begins the steady beating
of wool into a trellis of colors
I am soothed by the rhythm
of her hands,
the swing of her body.

I lay alongside the loom
like once alongside my mother's piano
and listen to its cadence
and meter
and feel the great sides shake
with the gain.

We speak softly
like the shuttle
sliding so smooth across the warp
our dreams,
the day
detailed
gently
in the weave.

## About the Author

John Bates is the author of seven books and a contributor to seven others, all of which focus on the natural history of the Northwoods. He's worked as a naturalist in Wisconsin's Northwoods for three decades, leading an array of trips all designed to help people further understand the remarkable diversity and beauty of nature, and our place within it. John won the 2006 Ellis/Henderson Outdoor Writing Award from the Council for Wisconsin Writers for his book *Graced by the Seasons: Fall and Winter in the Northwoods*. His poetry has appeared in five collaborative art and science exhibits, and has been published in various journals including *Oxford Magazine*, *Wisconsin Academy Review*, *Albatross*, and *The Northern Review*. John also presents talks and programs throughout the Lakes States on subjects from "A Spirit of Place" to "Winter Ecology." See *www.manitowish.com*.

John and his wife Mary live in northern Wisconsin in Mary's grand-parent's home where they raised two daughters.

## About the Weaver

Mary Burns expresses her love of northern woodlands and waters in her weavings and writings. An award-winning weaver, she has displayed her work in many art exhibits and shows, and her work resides in private homes across the United States.

As a jacquard weaver, she designs uniquely complex, detailed fiber art images based on the natural world, historical photos, or her own pastel paintings. From her designs, she then creates separate weaving structures for each shade of color, allowing her to "paint" with yarn. She weaves these pieces by hand with cotton yarns, blending two to four threads per shuttle to achieve the right color. This highly technical weaving process allows her to marry modern weaving techniques to the timeless world of forest and water.

In her latest work, *Ancestral Women Exhibit: Wisconsin's 12 Tribes,* Mary honors women's journeys by creating their portraits in jacquard weavings. The *Ancestral Women* project was conceived to portray the strength of ancestral women around the world, both elders and their contemporaries. The first phase of this larger project features women elders from each of Wisconsin's 12 Native American tribes. Mary also wove six clan pieces and four landscape pieces for the exhibit that illustrate essential cultural practices. See *www.ancestralwomen.com.*

# PRAISE FOR JOHN BATES' WRITINGS

## A Northwoods Companion (two volume set)

*Bates would seem the perfect companion in the outdoors, the sort of fellow that could turn an ordinary walk into a graduate course.*

- *Milwaukee Journal Sentinel*

*It would be equally enjoyable to slip this book in your backpack with your sandwich and field guides, take it along when you can sneak in ten minutes of reading between appointments, or keep it on your nightstand for a few minutes of quality reading at the end of the day.*

- *Wisconsin Natural Resources Magazine*

## Graced by the Seasons (two volume set)

*Graced by the Seasons: Fall and Winter takes us on a fascinating trip through the Northwoods highlighting the many wonders of the outdoors. In his typical easy readable style, Bates presents both every day occurrences and complex mysteries of nature in a way that demonstrates our intimate bond with the world outside our windows.*

- Dr. Mike Dombeck, Chief Emeritus, U.S. Forest Service

*Anyone with a passion for nature will find this book a great addition to their collection whether for reading in a tent or for next to one's favorite chair. The beauty and mystery of the world around us is captured beautifully.*

- Rob McKim, Central Region Director for The Nature Conservancy

## River Life: The Natural and Cultural History of a Northern River

*An excellent resource for presenting examples of natural history and ecology or for highlighting the biodiversity of northern temperate rivers . . . Bates leads the way with tantalizing stories.*

- *Choice*, Current Reviews for Academic Libraries

*A thousand thanks for a copy of your handsome River Life . . . It's an honorable piece of work . . . a treat to read.*

- Ann Zwinger, author of 21 books and winner of the John Burroughs Medal

## Trailside Botany

*Bates crafts his language to reflect the beauty he sees in each plant. Trailside Botany is as lively and diverse as a patch of woods.*

*- The Minnesota Conservation Volunteer*

*This book is a perfect addition to any hiker's backpack. Written in easy-to-understand language, it is a natural for everyone who loves the outdoors.*

- The Nature Conservancy, Minnesota Chapter

## Seasonal Guide to the Natural Year for Minnesota, Michigan, and Wisconsin

*There are the rare outdoor books that are so jam-packed with interesting stuff that you find yourself reaching for it whenever you get a spare minute to yourself . . . you pick it up as much for the pleasure as you do for the information. Wisconsin outdoor writer John Bates has just published such a book.*

- Russell King, Council for Wisconsin Writers

CPSIA information can be obtained
at www.ICGtesting.com
Printed in the USA
FFOW03n1109230118
44603567-44503FF